FOOTBALL HANDBOOK

Scholastic Children's Books
Euston House, 24 Eversholt Street,
London NW1 1DB, UK

A division of Scholastic Ltd
London ~ New York ~ Toronto ~ Sydney ~ Auckland
Mexico City ~ New Delhi ~ Hong Kong

First published in the UK by Scholastic Ltd as *Epic Football Expert*, 2016
This updated edition published by Scholastic Ltd, 2019

Written by Kevin Pettman
Updated by Sara Stanford
© Scholastic Children's Books, 2016, 2019

ISBN 978 1407 19170 6

Printed in China

2 4 6 8 10 9 7 5 3 1

Papers used by Scholastic Children's Books are made from wood grown in sustainable forests.

www.scholastic.co.uk

CONTENTS

CHAPTER ONE

Which Player Are You Like? 6
The History of Football 9
How Football Kicked Off 10
Football Rules 12
Positions & Players 14
How Competitions Work 16
Football Words & Phrases 18
Footy Rules Quiz 20
Spot the Difference 21
Epic Moments 22

CHAPTER TWO

Top Players 23
Top Female Players 36
Footy Legends 40
Top Players Quiz 42
Number Cruncher 43
Epic Moments 44

CHAPTER THREE

Top 10 Teams 45
Top 5 Women's Teams 52
Top Team Quiz 54
Looking for Legends Wordsearch 55
Epic Moments 56

CHAPTER FOUR

Competitions 57
English Premier League 58
Spanish La Liga 60
FIFA Women's World Cup 62
Italian Serie A 64
European Champions League 66
English FA Cup 68
FIFA World Cup 70
South American Copa America 72
European Championship 74
More Top Competitions 76
Competitions Quiz 78
Epic Moments 80

CHAPTER FIVE

Top 10 Stadiums 81
Top 10 Stadiums Quiz 88
Final Footy Quiz 90
Footy Wordsearch 91
Epic Moments 92

Answers 93
Index 94

WHICH PLAYER ARE YOU LIKE?

Take this fun quiz to see which footballer you're like. Make your decision and follow each white line — then turn over the page to see your football hero.

GOALS

Would you like to score lots of goals or show off your tricks with the ball?

FOOTY FACT!

In 1991, Germany legend Lothar Matthäus was the first player to win the World Player of the Year award.

TRICKS

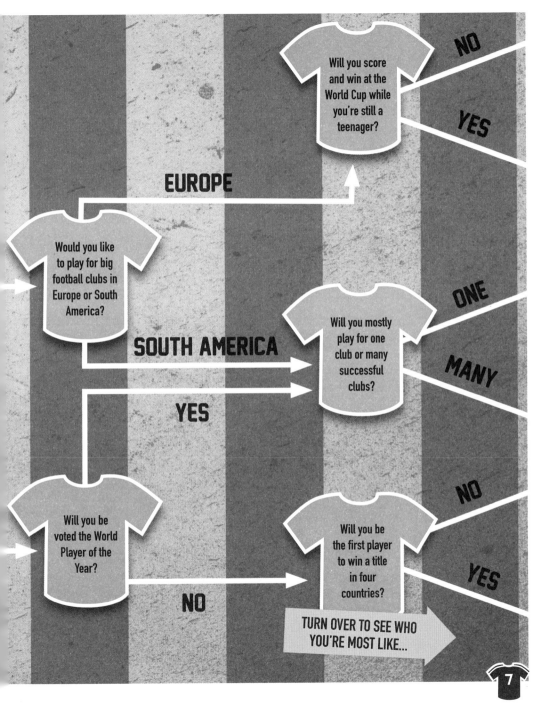

Will you score and win at the World Cup while you're still a teenager?

NO

YES

EUROPE

Would you like to play for big football clubs in Europe or South America?

SOUTH AMERICA

Will you mostly play for one club or many successful clubs?

ONE

MANY

YES

Will you be voted the World Player of the Year?

Will you be the first player to win a title in four countries?

NO

YES

NO

TURN OVER TO SEE WHO YOU'RE MOST LIKE...

7

NO

YES

ONE

MANY

NO

YES

KELLY SMITH

Kelly's power, strength and eye for a pass made her one of the best footballers of all time. A true leader, she demanded respect from her teammates and went on to win five FA cups with Arsenal.

PELÉ

Pelé is Brazil's greatest player, winning the World Cup when he was just seventeen and scoring over 1,000 goals in his career. Fans loved watching the talented striker in action in the 1950s, '60s and '70s.

ZLATAN IBRAHIMOVIĆ

One of the most entertaining players you could imagine, Zlatan is full of clever skills and can score stunning goals from all over the pitch. He became an icon wearing the No. 10 shirt for Sweden.

DAVID BECKHAM

Famous for creating goals and his ace free kicks, England captain Beckham won trophies with Manchester United, Real Madrid, LA Galaxy and Paris Saint-Germain.

THE
HISTORY
OF
FOOTBALL

Football has been around for a long time, with the rules of the game established in the nineteenth century. So before a football expert can find out about the modern-day superstars, they need to step back in time and see how the game developed, what positions there are on a football pitch, what the referee does, how competitions work . . . and more!

HOW
FOOTBALL

Games like football date back to ancient China, Greece and Rome. By the sixteenth century, a type of football was played in English schools but the rules differed, making it hard for teams to play each other. In 1848 at Cambridge University, the first 'laws' of the game were devised and in 1863, The Football Association revised them to create the sport we know.

1888

In this year, the world's first national football league was formed in England. These twelve clubs made up the league...

- Accrington
- Aston Villa
- Blackburn Rovers
- Bolton Wanderers
- Burnley

Preston North End were the first Football League champions. The team was undefeated in twenty-two games.

- Derby County
- Everton
- Notts County
- Preston North End
- Stoke
- West Bromwich Albion
- Wolverhampton Wanderers

FOOTY FACT!

A penalty kick was originally called 'the kick of death' when it was introduced to the laws of the game in 1891.

LAWS OF THE GAME

Fourteen laws were agreed in the 1860s, and they haven't changed much in the last 150 years. The current seventeen laws cover these areas...

1. The Field of Play
2. The Ball
3. The Number of Players
4. The Players' Equipment
5. The Referee
6. The Assistant Referee
7. The Duration of the Match
8. The Start and Restart of Play
9. The Ball In and Out of Play
10. The Method of Scoring
11. Offside
12. Fouls and Misconduct
13. Free Kicks
14. The Penalty Kick
15. The Throw-in
16. The Goal Kick
17. The Corner Kick

Dick, Kerr Ladies F.C. was established in 1917, made up of women working at a World War One munitions factory. Their matches drew in huge crowds — but some people felt it wasn't a suitable thing for them to be doing. In 1921 the FA banned women from playing in stadiums. The ban wouldn't lift until 1971, fifty years later.

THE FIRST SUPERSTAR

Stanley Matthews, called the 'Wizard of the Dribble' due to his speed and skill, is said to be football's first superstar. He played for Stoke and Blackpool from 1932 to 1965, until he retired at fifty.

THE GAME GOES GLOBAL

With the modern rules of football established, it didn't take long for the game's popularity to spread around the world. European and South American clubs became very strong with fantastic players, often inspired by English coaches and traditions.

FOOTY FACT!

The first official game between two countries was in 1872, when Scotland and England played out a 0–0 draw in Glasgow.

FOOTBALL RULES

The rules of football are quite simple. Two teams of eleven players compete, with the winner being the team who score the most goals in the game. Adult games last for ninety minutes and are made up of two forty-five minute 'halves'. Youth games can be played for a shorter time. At half-time, the teams switch directions and try to score in the other goal.

THE REFEREE

A referee runs around, staying near to the ball, to make sure players play by the rules. The referee blows a whistle if a team or player breaks a rule and can award free kicks, penalties or dismiss players. In some professional games, the 'ref' is helped by as many as five assistants around the pitch.

FOUL PLAY

The referee or assistants can call a foul and temporarily stop the game if a football law has been broken. This could be if a player illegally tackles an opponent, plays dangerously, acts inappropriately or obstructs the ball.

SCORING GOALS

If all of the ball crosses the goal line, a goal has been scored. Most goals happen when the ball is kicked or headed past the goalkeeper, but goals can be scored with any part of the body apart from hands and arms.

YELLOW AND RED CARDS

The referee awards a free kick to the indignant team for minor fouls, but for more serious or persistent fouls the ref can award a card. If a player gets two yellow cards, he or she must leave the game. A red card means the player also leaves the game immediately.

FOOTY FACT!

David Beckham became the first player to get two red cards while playing international football for England. David was 'red-carded' at the 1998 World Cup finals in France, then was given a red card in a game against Austria in 2005. Wayne Rooney also picked up red cards with England, in 2006 and 2011.

OFFSIDE RULE

Probably the most complicated football rule! A player is offside if they are in the other team's half and nearer to the goal line than the ball and the second-to-last opponent. The goalkeeper is usually the last opponent. A goal can't be scored by a player who is offside and an official will signal this and award a free kick.

POSITIONS & PLAYERS

The eleven players all play in a certain position. The goalkeeper is the only player allowed to catch and handle the ball, apart from when other players take a throw-in. The goalkeeper's job is to stop the ball going into their goal. The right-back and left-back are defenders and focus on stopping the other team attacking. The two centre-backs spend most of the game in their half, tackling opponents, heading the ball and passing to the midfielders and strikers. The left-winger, right-winger and central midfielders have to attack and defend the ball and are often quick and skilful players. The two strikers try to score goals for the team, but any of the players can score a goal.

SUBSTITUTES

In a normal competitive game, the team manager can make up to three changes to the team at any time. A substitute player replaces one of the players that started the game.

SHIRT NUMBERS

Players can wear any number on their shirt. Traditionally the goalkeeper has number one and defenders use two, three, five and six. The midfielders wear four, eight, seven and eleven and the strikers wear numbers nine and ten.

TACTICS

A team must have one goalkeeper, but they could play with five defenders, three midfielders and two strikers — or any other combination! The most popular formation is '4-4-2' with four defenders, four midfielders and two strikers.

PITCH SIZE

The size of the football pitch can vary from youth to professional level. It must be rectangular and between 90 and 120 metres long and 45 to 90 metres wide. A full-size goal is 2.44 metres high and 7.32 metres wide.

FOOTY FACT!

Some teams, such as Barcelona and Bayern Munich, have played without a recognized striker. Attacking midfielders switch around and act as a 'false number nine' striker during the game.

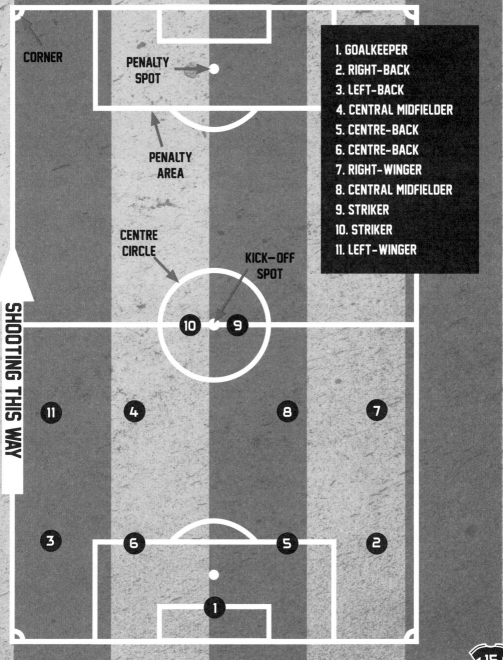

CORNER

PENALTY SPOT

PENALTY AREA

CENTRE CIRCLE

KICK-OFF SPOT

SHOOTING THIS WAY

1. GOALKEEPER
2. RIGHT-BACK
3. LEFT-BACK
4. CENTRAL MIDFIELDER
5. CENTRE-BACK
6. CENTRE-BACK
7. RIGHT-WINGER
8. CENTRAL MIDFIELDER
9. STRIKER
10. STRIKER
11. LEFT-WINGER

HOW COMPETITIONS WORK

Every country will have its own football league. There are usually between eighteen and twenty-four teams in a league and each team will play each other twice in a season — once at each other's ground. The winner of a game collects three points and if the game is a draw each team gets one point. You get no points for losing a game. The team with the most points after all the games have been played is the league champion. Below is the Premier League table for the 2017–18 season.

	Pld	W	D	L	Pts
1 Manchester City	38	32	4	2	100
2 Manchester United	38	25	6	7	81
3 Tottenham Hotspur	38	23	8	7	77
4 Liverpool	38	21	12	5	75
5 Chelsea	38	21	7	10	70
6 Arsenal	38	19	6	13	63
7 Burnley	38	14	12	12	54
8 Everton	38	13	10	15	49
9 Leicester City	38	12	11	15	47
10 Newcastle United	38	12	8	18	44
11 Crystal Palace	38	11	11	16	44
12 Bournemouth	38	11	11	16	44
13 West Ham United	38	10	12	16	42
14 Watford	38	11	8	19	41
15 Brighton and Hove Albion	38	9	13	16	40
16 Huddersfield Town	38	9	10	19	37
17 Southampton	38	7	15	16	36
18 Swansea City	38	8	9	21	33
19 Stoke City	38	7	12	19	33
20 West Bromich Albion	38	6	13	19	31

Pld = games played W = games won D = games drawn L = games lost Pts = points won

CUP COMPETITIONS

Cup competitions, such as the FA Cup and Coppa Italia in Italy, play in the format where the winning team goes through to the next round. A 'draw' will take place where teams are randomly picked to play each other — so small teams from a lower league can play against bigger teams. Some cup games can be played in two 'legs' with the 'aggregate' winner (the team that scores the most goals overall) going through, or thirty minutes extra-time can even be played if the score is tied at the end of normal play.

GROUP STAGES

The Champions League and Europa League are cup competitions, but they also have a group stage at the beginning. Groups of four teams play each other twice — home and away — with the two top teams after six games going through to the knockout games. This means that a team could lose a game in the group stage, but still go on to win the cup!

PLAY-OFFS

The English Football League uses a play-off system to decide who is promoted to the league above at the end of the season. The teams finishing between third and sixth, or fourth and seventh in League 2, play a knockout game. The winner of each goes to the play-off final, with that winner finally being promoted. It's an exciting system that gives lots of teams a reason to keep winning until the end of the season.

INTERNATIONAL TOURNAMENTS

For international tournaments, countries have to qualify to reach them. That means they play home and away against a number of other countries, with the teams at the top of the group making the tournament. Competitions such as the World Cup have a group stage and then knockout games to find the winner. When France won the World Cup in 2018, they played seven games at the finals.

WORDS & PHRASES

If you're going to be a football expert, you'll need to know what some of the weird words and phrases used in the sport actually mean.

HAT-TRICK: when a player scores three goals in one game it's called a hat-trick. It's nothing to do with a real hat though!

HIT THE NET: a phrase used to describe someone scoring a goal, because the ball has 'hit the back of the net'.

GOLDEN BOOT: when a player is the top scorer in a particular competition, the trophy they win is often called the Golden Boot.

PLAYMAKER: if a player is described as a playmaker, it means they are a creative player and like to set up and score goals for the team.

WING WIZARD: a footballer who plays in a wide position as a winger and has lots of skill. The phrase is often connected to the word 'dribbling'.

SKIPPER: skipper is another name for the captain of a football team. This player wears a captain's armband and makes many decisions for the team.

FOOTY FACT!

The manager of a football team trains the players, picks which players will play, decides team tactics and can make changes and substitutions during a game. The manager can be known as the 'boss', the 'coach' or the 'gaffer' but he or she is the main person in charge at a club.

DRIBBLING: running and keeping the ball at your feet and under control is called dribbling. Note: no babies involved!

KICK-OFF: this describes when a game begins and one team 'kicks off' the game by passing to someone else on their team.

LONG BALL: if a team plays in a long ball style, it means they will kick the ball high and forward a lot to put pressure on the other team's goal.

★ FOOTY RULES QUIZ ★

Now that you know the basic rules and guides to football, have a go at this fun quiz!

GAME OVER

Choose the right answer from the list of numbers we have given you.

1. How long extra-time will be played for in a cup competition. _____
2. This is the length of a normal game of professional football. _____
3. How long a goalkeeper can keep a ball in his or her hands for, before releasing it and starting play again. _____

A. SIX SECONDS   B. 30 MINUTES   C. 90 MINUTES

SHIRT SWAP

Write down which shirt number traditionally goes with these positions.
Take a sneak peek back at page 15 if you need help!

GOALKEEPER	____
RIGHT-BACK	____
CENTRE-BACK	____
CENTRE-BACK	____
LEFT-BACK	____
RIGHT-WINGER	____
CENTRAL MIDFIELDER	____
CENTRAL MIDFIELDER	____
LEFT-WINGER	____
STRIKER	____
STRIKER	____

SPOT THE DIFFERENCE

Check out England and Wales giving it everything they've got!
Can you spot six changes to the picture at the bottom?

Answers on page 93

EPIC MOMENTS

What? Germany beating Brazil 7–1

When? July 2014

Germany celebrate their historic 7–1 World Cup semi-final win against Brazil. Brazil, the host country of the tournament, were totally embarrassed by an amazing German team and the result made shock sporting headlines around the world.

TOP PLAYERS

The most important part of football (apart from having a ball to play with!) is the players. From children playing in the park to amateurs in their local teams and World Cup superstars — the players are what make football so special and so entertaining. It's now time to reveal the top players on the planet and their incredible skills...

20 SERGIO AGÜERO

Position: striker
Date of birth: 2 June 1988
Clubs: Man City, Atlético Madrid, Independiente, Argentina
Country: Argentina
Top skills: dribbling past defenders, finding space and scoring bags of goals
Famous for: scoring the goals to win City's first Premier League

Awesome Agüero joined Man City in 2011 and is easily their best player this century. His sharp skills in and around the box saw him rack up ninety Premier League goals in just 136 games, leading City to the title in 2012 and 2014. Sergio's strong for a little guy, is full of energy and forms a deadly duo with Lionel Messi in Argentina's attack.

19 LUKA MODRIĆ

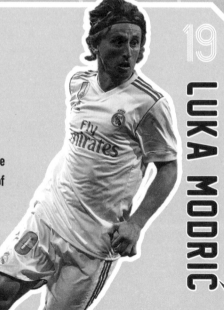

Position: central midfield
Date of birth: 9 September 1985
Clubs: Real Madrid, Croatia
Country: Croatia
Top skills: dribbling, accurate passing
Famous for: winning the Champions League four times

Modrić started out playing for Tottenham Hotspur before transferring to Real Madrid in 2012. He's now captain of the Croatia national team, too! This star is known for being a great team player who delivers passes with precision and has an ability to intersect in the most vital moments. Modrić is one to watch closely on the pitch!

24

Position: forward
Date of birth: **20 December 1998**
Clubs: **Paris Saint-Germain, France**
Country: **France**
Top skills: **speed, dribbling skills and goal scoring**
Famous for: **being the youngest player in thirty years to score ten Ligue 1 goals. Nice work!**

Did you know that Mbappé was the second most expensive Association Football transfer? He moved to Paris Saint-Germain from Monaco in 2018 for a whopping £128 million. Wowzer! This rising star has already earned himself a reputation as a highly skilled, mature and ambitious player. And what's more, he's even been dubbed the new Thierry Henry – not bad, eh?

18
KYLIAN MBAPPÉ

Position: **central** midfield
Date of birth: **4 January 1990**
Clubs: **Real Madrid**
Country: **Germany**
Top skills: **passing, long shots**
Famous for: **he helped lead Germany to a World Cup in 2014**

Meet Real Madrid's world-class midfielder, Toni Kroos! He made a good move when he swapped Munich for Madrid, and since then his career has gone from strength to strength. In fact, it's pretty hard to find fault in the young player. Kroos is hardworking and hugely talented, and this has gained him a lot of respect and a lot of trophies, too – including the Champions League (twice!) and La Liga 2016/17.

17
TONI KROOS

16

ISCO

Position: attacking midfielder
Date of birth: 21 April 1992
Clubs: Real Madrid
Country: Spain
Top skills: agility, possession of the ball and precision passing
Famous for: being described as one of the best attacking midfielders in the world

Isco kick-started his football career at Valencia, where he mostly played for the reserve team. He stuck at it until he was so good that none other than Real Madrid wanted him! In 2017 La Liga, Isco was the joint top scorer for Madrid. It's hardly surprising that Isco was handed a five-year deal in September 2017. He's not a player that anyone would want to lose, that's for sure!

15

GIANLUIGI BUFFON

Position: goalkeeper
Date of birth: 28 January 1978
Clubs: Juventus, Parma, Paris Saint-Germain
Country: Italy
Top skills: smart reflexes, catching crosses and being brave inside the penalty area
Famous for: playing over 150 games for Italy

Buffon became the world's most expensive keeper when he joined Juventus for £32 million in 2001, but he's still one of the best at forty years old. A calm figure between the goalposts and still setting clean-sheet records in 2016, Buffon has played in World Cup and Champions League finals and has won more than fifteen trophies playing in Italy.

Position: defender
Date of birth: 30 March 1986
Clubs: Real Madrid
Country: Spain
Top skills: tough tackling, strength on the ball and awesome heading
Famous for: winning the World Cup and Champions League

Ramos is a fierce defender – he's had more than 200 yellow and red cards in his career – but any team would pick him. He's not scared to head the ball, he commands his penalty area and has the speed and power to stop most attacks. He can also pop up with a goal, having scored over fifty goals for Real Madrid.

14 SERGIO RAMOS

Position: forward
Date of birth: 14 February 1987
Clubs: Paris Saint-Germain, Uruguay
Country: Uruguay
Top skills: fast pace, strong and powerful, with excellent ball posession
Famous for: being ranked 10th greatest player in the world by the *Guardian* newspaper in 2012

He moved to Paris Saint-Germain in 2013 after three years with Napoli. He is speedy, with strong header skills, and he can deliver great long shots! What's more, this player has serious possession skills when it comes to holding onto that ball – he just won't give it up for anyone. Is there anything he can't do?

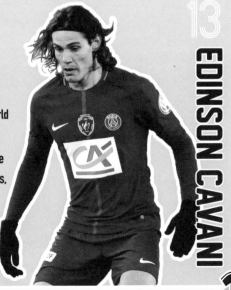

13 EDINSON CAVANI

12 EDEN HAZARD

Position: midfielder
Date of birth: 7 January 1991
Clubs: Chelsea, Lille, Belgium
Country: Belgium
Top skills: dribbling, taking penalties and whipping crosses into the box
Famous for: scoring twenty-eight Premier League goals in two seasons

Belgium midfielder Eden Hazard is exactly what his name suggests — a big hazard for goalkeepers and defenders! In his first two seasons at Chelsea he scored over thirty goals, winning the Premier League and Player of the Season in 2015. Eden is quick and strong and will dribble towards the goal from his wide attacking position. He is very accurate with free kicks as well.

11 PAULO DYBALA

Position: forward
Date of birth: 15 November 1993
Clubs: Juventus, Argentina
Country: Argentina
Top skills: long shots, dribbling, key passes and direct free kicks
Famous for: his two strikes that led to a 3-0 win to Juventus against Barcelona

Is he the next Lionel Messi? Well, plenty of people think so. Paulo Dybala quickly made his mark as one of the most exciting forwards out there! He signed with Juventus in 2015 and ended his first season as their leading scorer with twenty-three goals across all competitions.

Position: midfielder
Date of birth: 28 June 1991
Clubs: Manchester City, Wolfsburg, Bremen, Chelsea, Genk
Country: Belgium
Top skills: setting up goals, passing and finding space
Famous for: costing City a mega £55 million

Man City spent a club-record £55 million on the tricky Belgian in 2015, but that was a wise investment given the midfield skills and goals that he brings. Kevin De Bruyne is a class act — he rarely loses the ball, he is always looking to make a forward pass and delivers quality crosses into the box for the strikers.

10 KEVIN DE BRUYNE

Position: goalkeeper
Date of birth: 7 November 1990
Clubs: Manchester United, Spain
Country: Spain
Top skills: agility, quick reactions and punching the ball
Famous for: being the Man United Players' Player of the Year

Widely regarded as the Premier League's best shot-stopper, it's no wonder Real Madrid first tried to buy him in the summer of 2015. De Gea has that perfect mix of strength, agility, reactions, kicking and catching and there's little doubt that he will be Spain's No. 1 keeper for many years.

9 DAVID DE GEA

8

N'GOLO KANTÉ

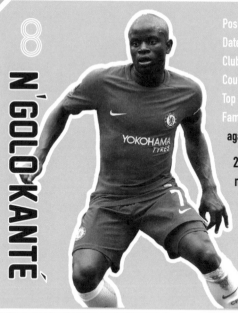

Position: midfielder
Date of birth: 29 March 1991
Clubs: Chelsea, France
Country: France
Top skills: energy, accurate passing and tough tackling skills
Famous for: scoring the only goal of an FA Cup quarter-final against Man Utd in 2016.

2017 was quite a year for energetic defensive midfielder, N'Golo Kanté! First, he was named *France Football*'s French Player of the Year and then Premiere League Player of the Season for Chelsea! If that wasn't enough, he was also named PFA Players' Player of the Year and FWA Footballer of the Year. Phew! Told you it was a good year for Kanté, didn't we?

7

MARCELO

Position: defender, left-wing attacker
Date of birth: 12 May 1988
Clubs: Real Madrid, Brazil
Country: Brazil
Top skills: nimble footwork, passing and crossing, tackling and interception, playing with the ball off the ground
Famous for: being included in FIFA's Pro Team of the Season for the third time in a row

Real Madrid sure have a lot to thank their defender, Marcelo, for. For starters, he helped his club keep the Champions League! He mostly plays at left-back, but can also play as left-winger and he is fast becoming one of Real Madrid's most powerful and influential players. We can't wait to see what the future holds for this superstar player.

Position: striker
Date of birth: 21 August 1988
Clubs: Bayern Munich, Dortmund, Lech Poznan, Znicz Pruszków
Country: Poland
Top skills: great strength, accurate shooting and powerful heading
Famous for: scoring five goals in just nine minutes in 2015

The big Poland international has been a red-hot striker for several years in Germany, scoring 116 goals in his first 198 Bundesliga games. He has great footwork and can lay the ball off to his teammates, but it's inside the penalty box where he is such a threat. Lewandowski's a natural goalscorer and could probably hit the net with his eyes closed!

6 ROBERT LEWANDOWSKI

Position: striker
Date of birth: 28 July 1993
Clubs: Tottenham, Leicester (loan), Norwich (loan), Millwall (loan), Leyton Orient (loan), England
Country: England
Top skills: powerful shooting, strength, calm finishing in the penalty box

Kane's breakthrough season came in 2014–15, when he suddenly started scoring for Tottenham and finished with thirty-two goals in all competitions. Strong, quick and skilful, he has the ability to shoot — and score — from a distance, but Kane can also beat defenders and surge into the penalty area. Kane was awarded the Golden Boot for scoring the most goals in the 2018 World Cup.

5 HARRY KANE

NEYMAR

Captain of the Brazil team when he was just 22, Neymar is such an exciting player to watch. He changed from being a showboating striker into an awesome part of Barça's front three, playing wide to pick up the ball or surging into the box to finish a flowing move. His unique flare and talent is admired worldwide and in 2017 he was signed by Paris Saint-Germain for an enormous fee of £200 million.

Position: striker
Date of birth: 5 February 1992
Clubs: Paris Saint-Germain, Brazil
Country: Brazil
Top skills: slick tricks, speed and clever link-up play
Famous for: being in Barcelona's MSN – Messi, Suárez, Neymar – strike force

FOOTY FACT!

Neymar actually rejected the chance to join Barcelona great rivals, Real Madrid, when he was fourteen.

LUIS SUÁREZ

Suárez's £75 million move to Barcelona from Liverpool in 2014 has been a bargain for the Spanish giants. The Uruguay international was the best all-round striker on the planet in 2016, scoring and creating goals for fun as he linked up with Messi and Neymar in La Liga and the Champions League. He scored sixty-two goals in his first eighty-one games at Barcelona to prove his world-class talent. Suárez also struck fifty-three goals in 102 games for his country — that's more than a goal a game on average.

Position: striker
Date of birth: 24 January 1987
Clubs: Barcelona, Liverpool, Ajax, Groningen, Nacional, Uruguay
Country: Uruguay
Top skills: running behind defenders, setting up goals and sharp shooting
Famous for: Champions League success in his first Barça season

FOOTY FACT!

Suárez scored seventeen Champions League goals in his first thirteen European games for Barcelona.

CRISTIANO RONALDO

REAL MADRID

The goals, trophies and records keep coming for the powerful striker. In the 2015-16 season Ronaldo scored his 350th goal for Real Madrid, the 500th in his career and came second in the FIFA Ballon d'Or awards. He can score all sorts of goals, from simple tap-ins to long-range volleys and bullet-like headers and has been Real's top scorer for six seasons in a row. It's no wonder Cristiano is paid a reported £365,000 a week — he is worth every penny to his club.

Position: striker
Date of birth: 5 February 1985
Clubs: Real Madrid, Man United, Sporting Lisbon, Portugal
Country: Portugal
Top skills: awesome strength, fierce free kicks and laser-guided shooting
Famous for: becoming Real Madrid's record goalscorer

PORTUGAL

For his country, the statistics speak for themselves — Ronaldo has scored 85 goals in 153 games for Portugal ever since making his national debut as an eighteen-year-old in 2003. He became a teenage star at Euro 2004 and has since played at four World Cups and Euro 2008, Euro 2012 and Euro 2016. In 2012, the Portugal captain also became his country's record goalscorer and played his 100th international game. He rightly rivals Eusébio as the nation's greatest-ever player.

BARCELONA

Is there anything left to say about just how good Lionel Messi is? He has been crowned World Player of the Year a record five times, he is Barcelona's record goalscorer with over 500 strikes and has won over thirty trophies, including four Champions Leagues in just ten seasons. Little Leo has been at Barça for his whole career and the fans adore his superhuman skills. Come the day when he finally stops playing and hangs up his goal-crazy boots, Camp Nou could be flooded with tears!

LIONEL MESSI

Position: striker
Date of birth: 24 June 1987
Clubs: Barcelona, Argentina national team
Country: Argentina
Top skills: a lethal left foot, magical skills and superhero speed
Famous for: being the best in the world — and probably the best of all time

ARGENTINA

With an incredible sixty-five goals in his first 127 games for Argentina, Messi is nearing the status of the country's other great No. 10 — Diego Maradona. The only thing holding Messi back is that he didn't win the World Cup when Argentina reached the final in 2014. Still, his amazing ability has made him an icon and hero in South America, winning an Olympic Gold medal in China in 2008 and the FIFA World Youth Championships in 2005.

FOOTY FACT!

When he was eighteen, Messi was sent off just two minutes after coming on as a sub on his debut for Argentina.

TOP FEMALE PLAYERS

6 — LUCY BRONZE

Position: right-back
Date of birth: 28 October 1991
Clubs: Olympique Lyonnais, England
Country: England
Top skills: dribbling, relentless energy
Famous for: being the first England player chosen for the FIFPro Women's World XI, and scoring in the final for Manchester City who won the FA Cup

Lucy Bronze already has heaps of awards under her belt including PFA Women's Players' Player of the Year in 2014 and 2017, as well as the English FA's Player of the Year in 2015. Not bad! Since signing a three-year contract with Lyon last year, her career has gone from strength to strength. It's her dream to win the Champions League with them and if anyone can make it happen, it's Bronze!

5 — PERNILLE HARDER

Position: striker
Date of birth: 15 November 1992
Clubs: VfL Wolfsburg, Denmark
Country: Denmark
Top skills: goal scoring, instinct, tactics
Famous for: she was 2017's Women's World Player of the Year in the inaugural female version of the Goal 50 award

Harder made an impact during her international debut aged just sixteen when she scored a hat-trick in Denmark's 15-0 win over Georgia. Since then she's won Danish Football Player of the Year in 2015, and captained Denmark at Euro 2017 who were runner's up. It's hardly surprising that she's won Denmark's Player of the Year award for the past three years!

Position: striker
Date of birth: 10 September 1993
Clubs: Chicago Red Stars, Perth Glory, Australia
Country: Australia
Top skills: goal scoring
Famous for: top scorer in National Women's Soccer League (NWSL)

With an impressive forty-three goals, Kerr is the leading all-time goalscorer in the National Women's Soccer League in the United States! Her success was certainly appreciated by her fellow Australians who named Sam Young Australian of the Year 2018 — it doesn't get much better than that. Kerr likes to celebrate on the pitch with awesome backflips or a good old knee slide!

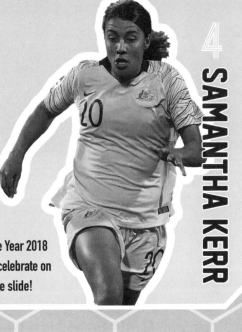

4 SAMANTHA KERR

Position: midfielder
Date of birth: 18 April 1992
Clubs: Olympique Lyonnais, Germany
Country: Hungary
Top skills: physically strong and can play either as a striker or a midfielder
Famous for: for scoring in the Olympic final at Rio 2016 when Germany beat Sweden 2-1

Football has been a huge part of Dzsenifer's life from day one, what with her father being the former Hungary midfielder Janos Marozsán. Dzsenifer was Bundesliga's youngest ever player when she made her debut at just fourteen in 2007. Ten years later and she was named Germany's Female Footballer of the Year 2017 — very well deserved after scoring in Rio 2016 against Sweden!

3 DZSENIFER MAROZSÁN

2

LIEKE MARTENS

Lieke Martens is a hugely successful Dutch international player with more than fifty caps under her belt. This speedy midfielder is known for her technical ability and top-notch goal scoring. During her career she has scored an amazing thirty-eight goals for the Netherlands, including the three infamous ones at the Euro 2017 final when they beat Denmark 4–2! Martens was named Best FIFA Women's Player in 2017 and UEFA Women's Player of the Year for 2016–17.

Position: midfielder
Date of birth: 16 December 1992
Clubs: FC Barcelona Femení, Netherlands
Country: Netherlands
Top skills: goal scoring, technical ability, speed, dribbling
Famous for: scoring three goals to help win Euro 2017 for
Netherlands and named Player of the Tournament

FOOTY FACT!

Alongside her football career, she's studying Spanish and taking a Masters in Sport Management!

We couldn't not dedicate this space to the awesome Carli Lloyd who paved the way for female footballers across the globe. She's a two-time Olympic gold medalist, and a FIFA Women's World Cup champion, as well as FIFA Player of the Year 2015 and 2016! Lloyd was famously the first person ever to score three goals in a FIFA Women's World Cup final, and the second player in history to score a hat-trick in any senior FIFA World Cup final.

CARLI LLOYD

Position: midfielder

Date of birth: 16 July 1982

Clubs: United States women's national soccer team

Country: United States

Top skills: goal scoring, finishing ability, creating opportunities

Famous for: scoring the fastest goal in FIFA World Cup final history, giving Team USA a 1-0 lead just two minutes and thirty-four seconds into the match.

FOOTY FACT!

Carli scored the gold medal-winning goals in the finals of the 2008 and the 2012 Summer Olympics.

FOOTY LEGENDS

You've seen the top current players in the world, but don't forget about these football legends of the past...

ARGENTINA | NAPOLI | STRIKER
Best moment: winning the 1986 World Cup
One of the game's greatest, Maradona was the hero of the '86 World Cup and took Napoli to two Italian titles. The skilful goalscorer also starred for Barcelona and Boca Juniors.

DIEGO MARADONA

ZINEDINE ZIDANE (aka Zizou)

FRANCE | REAL MADRID | MIDFIELDER
Best moment: scoring twice in the 1998 World Cup final
Fans talk about whether Zidane or Michel Platini is France's best-ever player, but 'Zizou' won the World Cup, European Championship and Champions League. He was a midfield maestro who could run a game with his passing and vision.

BRAZIL | REAL MADRID | STRIKER
Best moment: scoring eight goals at the 2002 World Cup
The Brazilian was a goal machine in his career — hitting the net for European giants like Barcelona, Inter Milan, Real Madrid and AC Milan. In 2002, he won the World Cup for a second time after scoring twice in the final.

RONALDO

JOHAN CRUYFF

HOLLAND | BARCELONA | MIDFIELDER

Best moment: winning three European Cups with Ajax

Cruyff was a majestic attacking midfielder for Ajax and Barcelona, winning trophies with both and leading Holland to the 1974 World Cup final. He was famous for his 'Cruyff turn' — a skill which left defenders trailing in his wake!

FOOTY FACT!

Johan Cruyff also managed Barcelona to four league titles in a row in the 1990s.

GERMANY | BAYERN MUNICH | STRIKER

Best moment: lifting the World Cup in 1974

Müller is a legend for Bayern Munich and Germany, scoring a staggering 365 goals in 427 Bundesliga games and sixty-two goals in sixty-eight games for Germany. Between 1974 and 1976 he shot Bayern to three European Cup wins in a row.

GERD MÜLLER

BOBBY

ENGLAND | MAN UNITED | MIDFIELDER

Best moment: winning the World Cup in 1966

Charlton helped Manchester United become the first English club to win the European Cup in 1968 and won three league championships with The Red Devils. For England he won the '66 World Cup and scored forty-nine goals for his country — not a bad goalscoring record for a midfielder!

TOP PLAYERS QUIZ

You're up to date on all the best players, so switch your footy brain on and answer these quick questions.

PICK A PLAYER

Choose the right name to answer these teasers from the list below.

1. Who has played for Tottenham, Leicester, Norwich, Millwall and Leyton Orient?

2. This classy star is the oldest player in the top players list.

3. This super striker is the only Hungarian player in the top players list.

A. LIEKE MARTENS   B. ROBERT LEWANDOWSKI   C. DZSENIFER MAROZSÁN

AWARD WINNER

One of the top players won *France Football*'s French Player of the Year in 2017.
Fill in the missing letters below to name the player.

N' _ _ _ _ K _ _ _ _

NUMBER CRUNCHER

Take a look at Barcelona's all time favourite trio of Messi, Suárez and Neymar.
But do YOU know which shirt number each of them wore?
Write the answer down.

SUÁREZ Nº _____

NEYMAR Nº _____

MESSI Nº _____

Answers on page 93

EPIC MOMENTS

What? England winning the World Cup final

When? July 1966

England captain Bobby Moore is paraded by his teammates after England win their first World Cup final. With the Jules Rimet Trophy in his hand, the crowd at Wembley cheered around him. The game finished 4–2 after going to extra time, but striker Geoff Hurst scored a hat-trick to seal the historic victory.

TOP 10 TEAMS

There are hundreds of professional football clubs from leagues all around the world. But which of these teams can truly be crowned the best? We reveal the facts, stats and stories that set these ten clubs ahead of the rest and why you should know about them in your quest to become a football expert!

BORUSSIA DORTMUND

10

Germany	COUNTRY
1909	YEAR FORMED
Robert Lewandowski, Marco Reus, André Schürrle	FAMOUS PLAYERS
Matthias Sammer, Jürgen Kohler, Michael Zorc	CLUB LEGENDS
£25.5 million for André Schürrle	MAX TRANSFER
Westfalenstadion	STADIUM
BVB	NICKNAME

Borussia Dortmund are the most successful club in Germany and eight-time Bundesliga champions. Their stadium is the largest in Germany and is named after its home region of Westphalia. The club has the highest average attendance of any association football club in the world.

LIVERPOOL FC

9

COUNTRY	England
YEAR FORMED	1892
FAMOUS PLAYERS	Philippe Coutinho, Daniel Sturridge
CLUB LEGENDS	Steven Gerrard, Ian Rush, Kenny Dalglish
MAX TRANSFER	£75 million for Virgil van Dijk
STADIUM	Anfield
NICKNAME	The Reds

With eighteen league titles, eleven major European cups and a host of domestic cup wins, Liverpool are well worth a spot in this top ten. Famed for their passing style of football and for producing homegrown players, pulling on their famous red shirt and running out at Anfield is a dream for many footballers.

46

8

COUNTRY	England
YEAR FORMED	1878
FAMOUS PLAYERS	Wayne Rooney, Anthony Martial, Chris Smalling
CLUB LEGENDS	George Best, Bobby Charlton, Eric Cantona
MAX TRANSFER	£89 million for Paul Pogba
STADIUM	Old Trafford
NICKNAME	The Red Devils

Winners of the first-ever Premier League season in 1993, Man United went on to rule English football over the next twenty years to win a record thirteen modern-day titles. With eleven FA Cups and three Champions Leagues, the biggest club stadium in the UK and millions of fans around the world, The Red Devils are worthy of the No. 8 position in the greatest clubs countdown!

7

France	COUNTRY
1970	YEAR FORMED
Neymar, Edinson Cavani, Thiago Silva	FAMOUS PLAYERS
Zlatan Ibrahimović, Ronaldinho	CLUB LEGENDS
£198 million for Neymar	MAX TRANSFER
Parc des Princes	STADIUM
PSG, or Les Parisiens (The Parisians)	NICKNAME

France's top club, Paris Saint-Germain, is a big player in European football and shows no sign of stopping! PSG's ever growing trophy count make it the most successful French football club in history. The star-studded club wear red and blue and play in the highest tier of French football, the Ligue 1.

47

6

SEVILLA FC

Spain	COUNTRY
1890	YEAR FORMED
Luis Muriel, Diego Maradona	FAMOUS PLAY...
Unai Emery	CLUB LEGENDS
£19 million for Luis Muriel	MAX TRANSFER
Ramón Sánchez Pizjuán Stadium	STADIUM
Sevillistas Los Rojiblancos (The White and Reds)	NICKNAME

Sevilla FC is Spain's oldest football club, but it's pretty hard to stand out when you're up against the likes of Barcelona and Real Madrid. Nevertheless, this determined club based in Seville has been home to big names and plenty of success over the years, including reaching the quarter finals of the 2018 Champions League.

5

JUVENTUS

COUNTRY	Italy
YEAR FORMED	1897
FAMOUS PLAYERS	Paul Pogba, Gianluigi Buffon, Paulo Dybala
CLUB LEGENDS	Alessandro Del Piero, Michel Platini, Zinedine Zidane
MAX TRANSFER	£75.3 million for Gonzalo Higuaín
STADIUM	Juventus Stadium
NICKNAME	The Old Lady

Italy's most famous and celebrated team, with a record 31 championships between 1905 and 2015, the black and white stripes of the Juventus kit is recognized the world over. In the 2010s they have dominated Serie A once again and reached the 2016 Champions League final — Juve's ninth European Cup final in total.

COUNTRY	Germany
YEAR FORMED	1900
FAMOUS PLAYERS	Robert Lewandowski, Arjen Robben, Thomas Müller
CLUB LEGENDS	Gerd Müller, Franz Beckenbauer, Lothar Matthäus
MAX TRANSFER	£36.5 million for Corentin Tolisso
STADIUM	Allianz Arena
NICKNAME	Bayern

4

Bundesliga, Champions League, UEFA Cup, UEFA Super Cup – German giants Bayern Munich have all these trophies and more on display at the Allianz Arena. They are the biggest, most successful and richest club in Germany and sell out their 75,000 capacity stadium in most games. Playing for, or even against Bayern, is a big occasion.

3

Spain	COUNTRY
1903	YEAR FORMED
Fernando Torres, Antoine Griezmann, Diego Godín	FAMOUS PLAYERS
Abelardo Fernández, Luis Aragonés, Radamel Falcao	CLUB LEGENDS
£63 million for Thomas Lemar	MAX TRANSFER
Vicente Calderón Stadium	STADIUM
Rojiblancos	NICKNAME

Atlético Madrid lives in the shadow of Real Madrid and Barcelona, but the famous Spanish club has a rich history of great players and winning trophies. Atlético were La Liga champions in 2014 and runners-up in the Champions League that year, too. In total the club has won over twenty-five major competitions.

49

2

Spain	COUNTRY
1899	YEAR FORMED
Lionel Messi, Luis Suárez, Neymar	FAMOUS PLAY
Xavi Hernández, Johan Cruyff, Ronaldinho	CLUB LEGENDS
£105 million for Philippe Coutinho	MAX TRANSFE
Camp Nou	STADIUM
Barça	NICKNAME

The *Football Handbook* award for one of the biggest and the best football teams in the world has to go to Barcelona. It's the home of the best player in the world (Lionel Messi of course!), the biggest stadium in Europe and the most thrilling squad of players this century. Barça fans have been treated to wonderful action and wonderful success over the last ten years.

Lionel Messi has been the player to transform Barcelona into the force they are now. Helped over the years by players like Ronaldinho, Xavi, Iniesta, Puyol and Eto'o, he is the symbol of the club and main reason they have won so much silverware since 2004. That blue and red kit is loved by tens of millions of fans all over the planet!

FOOTY FACT!

Barça won the Spanish Cup — called the Copa del Rey — a record thirty times between 1910 and 2018.

COUNTRY	Spain
YEAR FORMED	1902
~OUS PLAYERS	Cristiano Ronaldo, Sergio Ramos, Gareth Bale
CLUB LEGENDS	Raúl, Zinedine Zidane, Alfredo di Stéfano
~AX TRANSFER	£85 million for Gareth Bale
STADIUM	Santiago Bernabéu Stadium
NICKNAME	The Whites (Los Blancos)

1

FOOTY FACT!

Real Madrid paid £236 million in total for their attacking trio of Cristiano Ronaldo, Gareth Bale and James Rodríguez.

'Real' means royal in Spanish, and there's no doubting that Real Madrid is a majestic football club steeped in history and glory. Real hold the record for winning the Champions League trophy sixteen times, and its epic battles with arch rival Barcelona continue to attract fans the world over.

Zidane, Ronaldo, Raúl, Gento, Zárraga, Sánchez and Casillas are just some of the many legends connected to this great club. From setting world-record transfer fees to picking up the most prestigious trophies in Spain and abroad, having the chance to play for 'Los Blancos' is something very few players turn down.

REAL MADRID

TOP 5 WOMEN'S TEAMS

It's not just countries that compete for glory in the women's games — there are hundreds of professional domestic clubs too. This is the *Football Handbook* guide to our top five...

5 — CHELSEA LADIES FC

League: FA Women's Super League
Country: England
Year formed: 1992
Major trophies: 2 FA Women's Super League title, 2 FA Women's Cup titles
Star player: Katie Chapman
Did you know? Chelsea legend and captain John Terry is also the president of the Chelsea Ladies Football Team.

4 — FFC TURBINE POTSDAM

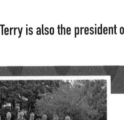
1. FFC TURBINE POTSDAM

League: Women's Bundesliga
Country: Germany
Year formed: 1971
Major trophies: 6 Women's Bundesliga titles, 2 Women's Champions League titles
Star player: Elise Kellond-Knight
Did you know? Potsdam won the league four years in a row between 2009 and 2012, beating their fierce rivals FFC Frankfurt.

3

ARSENAL LADIES FC

League: FA Women's Super League

Country: England

Year formed: 1987

Major trophies: 2 Women's Super League, 14 FA Women's Cups, 1 Women's Champions League

Star player: Kelly Smith

Did you know? Arsenal are the most successful women's team in England, winning 58 trophies — including a record 12 Premier League titles between 1993 and 2010.

2

OLYMPIQUE LYONNAIS

League: Division 1 Féminine

Country: France

Year formed: 2004

Major trophies: 16 Division 1 Féminine titles, 7 French Cups, 5 Women's Champions League titles

Star player: Ada Hegerberg

Did you know? Previously known as FC Lyon, the club won an impressive nine league titles in a row from 2007 to 2015.

1

FFC FRANKFURT

League: Women's Bundesliga

Country: Germany

Year formed: 1998

Major trophies: 7 Women's Bundesliga titles, 4 Women's Champions League titles

Star player: Kerstin Garefrekes

Did you know? Frankfurt won the first-ever Champions League in 2002 and have a record four wins in the event from six appearances in the final.

TOP TEAM QUIZ

You've discovered all the facts and stats about the best teams — now it's time to tackle these tricky tests!

NAME GAME

Rearrange these funny football phrases to spell a correct top team name (male or female)...

1
SPARE MAINS TINA

_____

2
EVIL LOP OR

_____

3
MADDER LIAR

_____

4
MACHINERY NUB

_____

5
CALENDAR FALSIES

_____

MATCH UP

Can you link the club to their nickname?

Manchester United	The Whites
Barcelona	Rojiblancos
Juventus	Barça
Real Madrid	The Red Devils
Atlético Madrid	The Old Lady

LOOKING FOR LEGENDS

These famous footballers all appeared for our top teams. Can you find them all in this wordsearch?

CHARLTON	DEL PIERO	RÁUL
CRUYFF	FALCAO	MARADONA
DALGLISH	HENRY	MÜLLER

M	U	L	L	N	Z	O	J	P	Y	C	C	M	A	B
A	A	S	P	F	A	K	O	X	L	Q	J	A	E	Z
R	E	B	W	R	V	R	Y	A	U	B	S	R	R	H
A	E	L	D	F	I	O	H	D	A	O	U	A	Z	M
G	R	U	Y	I	N	E	B	A	R	L	O	D	A	W
O	M	S	D	K	N	G	P	H	R	Q	F	O	N	D
K	U	E	F	R	X	I	V	D	U	D	E	N	N	A
W	L	A	Y	E	R	B	T	F	A	L	C	A	O	N
M	L	M	P	H	O	A	J	S	K	A	L	Z	T	O
R	E	Z	B	U	P	S	T	X	H	O	R	N	L	G
M	R	C	O	A	C	R	U	Y	F	F	Z	I	R	P
D	J	R	E	L	O	L	I	Z	A	U	F	G	A	E
W	F	X	H	S	I	L	G	L	A	D	O	E	H	L
O	H	R	L	Y	P	A	I	F	T	A	X	R	C	L
O	R	E	I	P	L	E	D	Q	O	Z	K	J	C	E

Answers on page 93

55

EPIC MOMENTS

What? Messi wins his fifth World Player of the Year award

When? January 2016

Barcelona megastar Lionel Messi shows off his 2015 World Player of the Year award, with his Barcelona teammates clapping behind him. Messi has won the award five times, in 2009, 2010, 2011, 2012 and 2015.

COMPETITIONS

The next 18 pages are packed with awesome info, fantastic facts, super stats and powerful pictures all about the biggest football competitions. From the English Premier League to the FIFA Women's World Cup, the FA Cup to the European Champions League — you will find all the epic stuff you need to know. So what are you waiting for? Turn over now!

ENGLISH
PREMIER LEAGUE

There are four professional football leagues in England and the Premier League is the highest level. It has twenty teams, which compete against each other between August and the following May.

WINNERS

From when the Premier League was created in 1992 and up to 2018, only six different clubs have won it. Manchester United have a record 13 titles.

CLUB	WINS	YEARS
Man United	🏆🏆🏆🏆🏆🏆🏆	1993, '94, '96, '97, '99, 2000, '01, '03, '07, '08, '09, '11, '13, '14
Chelsea	🏆🏆🏆🏆🏆	2005, '06, '10, '15 '17
Arsenal	🏆🏆🏆	1998, 2002, '04
Man City	🏆🏆🏆	2012, '14, '18
Blackburn	🏆	1995
Leicester	🏆	2016

WATCHED WORLDWIDE

The fast, exciting and unpredictable football that is played in the Premier League means it is very popular in the UK and all around the world. Games are watched on TV in over 200 territories and it's estimated that 643 million homes have access to Premier League games.

MEGA MONEY

Because the Premier League is so popular and so many fans pay to watch it, the twenty clubs have millions to spend on buying the best players. Each year, clubs spend huge amounts to make their team as strong as possible. Here are the top ten most expensive Premier League player transfers between 1992 and 2018...

1. Paul Pogba	£93.25 million	Juventus to Man United
2. Virgil van Dijk	£75 million	Southampton to Liverpool
3. Romelu Lukaku	£75 million	Everton to Man United
4. Ángel Di María	£59.7 million	Real Madrid to Man United
5. Aymeric Laporte	£57 million	Athletic Bilbao to Man City
6. Pierre-Emerick Aubameyang	£56.1 million	Borussia Dortmund to Arsenal
7. Álvaro Morata	£56 million	Real Madrid to Chelsea
8. Kevin De Bruyne	£54.5 million	Wolfsburg to Man City
9. Alexandre Lacazette	£52 million	Lyon to Arsenal
10. Naby Keïta	£52.75 million	RB Leipzig to Liverpool

FOOTY FACT!

Leicester City won the 2015-2016 Premier League with extraordinary odds of 5000-1.

FOOTY FACT!

Arsenal won the Premier League without being beaten in 2004 and a special gold version of the Premier League trophy was made.

GOALS GOALS GOALS

Alan Shearer, who played as a striker for Newcastle and Blackburn in the Premier League before retiring in 2006, is the top goalscorer in the competition's history with 260 goals.

SPANISH LA LIGA

★★★★★★ SPANISH ★★★★★★
LA LIGA

Since 2000, Spain's Primera Division — more commonly known as La Liga — has probably been the most entertaining league in the world. Most of the best players are there, with Barcelona and Real Madrid dominating the trophies.

WINNERS

CLUB	WINS	YEARS
Real Madrid	(33)	1932, '33, '54, '55, '57 '58, '61, '62, '63, '64, '65, '67, '68 '69, '72, '75, '76, '78, '79, '80, '86, '87, '88, '89, '90, '95, '97, 2001, '03, '07, '08, '12, '17
Barcelona	(25)	1929, '45, '48, '49, '52, '53, '59, '60, '74, '85, '91, '92, '93, '94, 98, '99, 2005, '06, '09, '10, '11, '13, '15, '16, '18
At. Madrid	(10)	1940, '41, '50, '51, '66, '70, '73, '77, '96, 2014
Ath. Bilbao	(8)	1930, '31, '34, '36, '43, '56, '83, '84
Valencia	(6)	1942, '44, '47, '71, 2002, '04
Real Sociedad	(2)	1981, '82
Deportivo	(1)	2000
Sevilla	(1)	1946
Real Betis	(1)	1935

FOOTY FACT!

La Liga was created in 1929 and only three founding clubs — Real Madrid, Barcelona and Athletic Bilbao — have never been relegated from the division in that time.

GOAL KINGS

La Liga is famous for attacking football and for celebrating strikers and goalscorers. Take a look at La Liga's top scorers each season so far this century...

Player	Season	Goals	Games
Raúl (Real Madrid)	2000–01	24	36
Diego Tristán (Deportivo)	2001–02	20	35
Roy Makaay (Deportivo)	2002–03	29	38
Ronaldo (Real Madrid)	2003–04	24	32
Diego Forlán (Villarreal)	2004–05	25	38
Samuel Eto'o (Barcelona)	2004–05	25	37
Samuel Eto'o (Barcelona)	2005–06	26	34
Ruud van Nistelrooy (R. Madrid)	2006–07	25	37
Dani Güiza (Real Mallorca)	2007–08	27	37
Diego Forlán (Atlético Madrid)	2008–09	32	33
Lionel Messi (Barcelona)	2009–10	34	35
Cristiano Ronaldo (Real Madrid)	2010–11	40	34
Lionel Messi (Barcelona)	2011–12	50	37
Lionel Messi (Barcelona)	2012–13	46	32
Cristiano Ronaldo (Real Madrid)	2013–14	31	30
Cristiano Ronaldo (Real Madrid)	2014–15	48	35
Luis Suárez (Barcelona)	2015–16	40	35
Lionel Messi (Barcelona)	2016–17	37	34
Lionel Messi (Barcelona)	2017–18	29	32

TITLE TALK

Real Madrid have the most La Liga titles and the player with the most individual league championships is Francisco Gento. Between 1954 and 1969 he won twelve titles playing with his famous Real Madrid team.

FIFA
★ ★ ★ ★ ★ ★ ★ ★ ★ ★ ★ ★ ★ ★ ★ ★

WOMEN'S WORLD CUP

A relatively new competition, the Women's World Cup has already established itself as an amazingly entertaining tournament. Terrific tactics, perfect passes and top players ... this competition just keeps getting tougher, and more popular, each year!

WINNERS

The first Women's World Cup was held in 1991 in China. The tournament is held every four years and between 1991 and 2015, the USA has been the most successful country with three World Cup victories.

CLUB	WINS	YEARS
USA	♛♛♛	1991, '99, 2015
Germany	♛♛	2003, '07
Norway	♛	1995
Japan	♛	2011

In 1991, only twelve teams competed, before the figure expanded to sixteen teams in 1999. In 2015, twenty-four teams competed, with Cameroon, Costa Rica, Côte d'Ivoire, Ecuador, Netherlands, Spain, Switzerland and Thailand playing for the first time. The next FIFA Women's World Cup is set for 2019, and once again twenty-four teams will compete.

GOAL QUEENS

Brazil striker Marta has scored a record fifteen goals at the finals. Only two players — Japan's Homare Sawa and Brazil's Formiga — have played at six finals in total. Check out this list of the top scorers.

Player	Goals	Games
Marta (Brazil)	15	17
Birgit Prinz (Germany)	14	24
Abby Wambach (USA)	14	25
Michelle Akers (USA)	12	13
Sun Wen (China)	11	20
Bettina Wiegmann (Germany)	11	22
Ann Kristin Aarønes (Norway)	10	11
Heidi Mohr (Germany)	10	12
Christine Sinclair (Canada)	9	17
Linda Medalen (Norway)	9	17
Hege Riise (Norway)	9	17

FOOTY FACT!

The 2015 Women's World Cup was the first football World Cup to be played on artificial turf.

TOP TROPHY

The FIFA Women's World Cup trophy has an original value of around £22,000. The cup itself has a green serpentine marble base, and the spiral and football are made with pure silver covered with 23-carat gold.

ITALIAN SERIE A

★ ★ ★ ★ ★ ★ ITALIAN ★ ★ ★ ★ ★ ★

SERIE A

Anyone who loves football has to love the Italian Serie A league! The strongest division in the 1980s and '90s, the world's greatest players such as Maradona, van Basten, Platini, Maldini and Zidane all showed off their silky skills for top Italian clubs.

WINNERS

CLUB	WINS	YEARS
Juventus	🏆🏆🏆🏆🏆🏆🏆🏆🏆🏆🏆🏆🏆🏆🏆🏆🏆🏆🏆🏆🏆🏆🏆🏆🏆🏆🏆🏆🏆🏆🏆🏆🏆🏆	1905, '26, '31–'35, '50, '52, '58, '60, '61, '67, 72, '73, '75, '77, '78, '81, '82, '84, '86, '95, '97, '98, 2002, '03, '12, '13, '14, '15, '16, '17, '18
AC Milan	🏆🏆🏆🏆🏆🏆🏆🏆🏆🏆🏆🏆🏆🏆🏆🏆🏆🏆	1901, '06, '07, 1951, '55, '57, '59, 1962, '68, 1979, 1988, 1992, '93, '94, '96, '99, 2004, 2011
Inter Milan	🏆🏆🏆🏆🏆🏆🏆🏆🏆🏆🏆🏆🏆🏆🏆🏆🏆🏆	1910, '20, '30, '38, '40, '53, '54, '63, '65, '66, '71, '80, '89, 2006, '07, '08, '09, '10
Genoa	🏆🏆🏆🏆🏆🏆🏆🏆🏆	1898, '99, '1900, '02, '03, '04, '15, '23, '24
Torino	🏆🏆🏆🏆🏆🏆🏆	1928, '43, '46, '47, '48, '49, '76
Bologna	🏆🏆🏆🏆🏆🏆🏆	1925, '29, '36, '37, '39, '41, '64
Pro Vercelli	🏆🏆🏆🏆🏆🏆🏆	1908, '09, '11, '12, '13, '21, '22
Roma	🏆🏆🏆	1942, '83, 2001
Lazio	🏆🏆	1974, 2000
Fiorentina	🏆🏆	1956, '69
Napoli	🏆🏆	1987, '90
Cagliari	🏆	1970

CLUB	WINS	YEARS
Casale	🏆	1914
Novese	🏆	1922
Verona	🏆	1985
Sampdoria	🏆	1991

RECORD BREAKERS

If you want to know a few quick-fire stats and facts about the legendary Italian league, then take a look at these slick Serie A snippets...

MOST SERIE A WINS IN ROW
Inter Milan, 27 (2006–10)

MOST SEASONS SPENT IN SERIE A
Internazionale, 87

SERIE A ALL-TIME TOP SCORER
Silvio Piola, 274 goals

LONGEST UNBEATEN RUN IN SERIE A
AC Milan, 58 games (1991–93)

MOST GOALS IN ONE SEASON
Gino Rossetti and Gonzalo Higuaín, 36 goals

MOST EXPENSIVE SERIE A TRANSFER
Hernán Crespo, £35.5m Parma to Lazio

MOST SERIE A GAMES
Paolo Maldini, 647 games

FOOTY FACT!

In 2016, Juventus keeper Gianluigi Buffon didn't concede a goal for a combined 974 minutes in Serie A.

EUROPEAN
CHAMPIONS LEAGUE

Is it the most prized silverware that a club can win? Lots of the big teams certainly think so and would probably rather win the Champions League than their own league. It's an incredibly prestigious trophy and every top star wants to get his hands on this big, shiny cup!

WINNERS

First called the European Cup before being renamed as the Champions League in 1992, this is the complete list of winners from 1955 (when the competition started) to 2018.

CLUB	WINS	YEARS
Real Madrid	♛♛♛♛♛♛♛♛♛♛♛♛♛	1956, '57, '58, '59, '60, '66, '98, 2000, '02, '14, '16, '17, '18
AC Milan	♛♛♛♛♛♛♛	1963, '69, '89, '90, '94, 2003, '07
Barcelona	♛♛♛♛♛	1992, 2006, '09, '11, '15
Liverpool	♛♛♛♛♛	1977, '78, '81, '84, 2005
Bayern Munich	♛♛♛♛♛	1974, '75, '76, 2001, '13
Ajax	♛♛♛♛	1971, '72, '73, '95
Man United	♛♛♛	1968, '99, 2008
Inter Milan	♛♛♛	1964, '65, 2010
Juventus	♛♛	1985, '96
Nottingham Forest	♛♛	1979, '80
Benfica	♛♛	1961, '62
Porto	♛♛	1987, 2004
PSV	♛	1988
Chelsea	♛	2012
Celtic	♛	1967

CLUB	WINS	YEARS
Hamburg	🏆	1983
Feyenoord	🏆	1979
Aston Villa	🏆	1982
Red Star Belgrade	🏆	1991
Borussia Dortmund	🏆	1997
Steaua Bucureşti	🏆	1986

GOAL KINGS

The competition has been around for over sixty years and only a handful of players have won it on several occasions. Here are ten of the best and the clubs they starred for.

PLAYER	NO. OF WINS	CLUB
Francisco Gento	6	Real Madrid
Alfredo di Stéfano	5	Real Madrid
José Maria Zárraga	5	Real Madrid
Rafael Lesmes	5	Real Madrid
Marquitos	5	Real Madrid
Juan Santisteban	5	Real Madrid
Juan Alonso	5	Real Madrid
Héctor Rial	5	Real Madrid
Paolo Maldini	5	AC Milan
Alessandro Costacurta	5	AC Milan

FOOTY FACT!

Glasgow Celtic were the first British team to win the European Cup in 1967.

ENGLISH
★ ★ ★ ★ ★ ★ ★ ★ ★ ★ ★ ★
FA CUP

As the oldest existing football competition in the world, the FA Cup is still a prize that every player in England wants to win. With the showpiece final at the famous Wembley Stadium, it's a big event in the world's football calendar.

WINNERS

CLUB	WINS	YEARS
Arsenal	★★★★★★★★★★★★★	1930, '36, '50, '71, '79, '93, '98, 2002, '03, '05, '14, '15, '1
Manchester United	★★★★★★★★★★★★	1909, '48, '63, '77, '83, '85, '90, '94, '96, '99, 2004, '16
Tottenham	★★★★★★★★	1901, '21, '61, '62, '67, '81, '82, '91
Chelsea	★★★★★★★★	1970, '97, '00, '07, '09, '10, '12, '18
Liverpool	★★★★★★★	1965, '74, '86, '89, '92, 2001, '06
Aston Villa	★★★★★★★	1887, '95, '97, 1905, '13, '20, '57
Newcastle	★★★★★★	1910, '24, '32, '51, '52, '55
Blackburn Rovers	★★★★★★	1884, '85, '86, '90, '91, 1928
Everton	★★★★★	1906, '33, '66, '84, '95
Manchester City	★★★★★	1904, '34, '56, '69, 2011
West Brom	★★★★★	1888, '92, 1931, '54, '68
Wanderers	★★★★★	1872, '73, '76, '77, '78
Sheffield United	★★★★	1899, 1902, '15, '25
Bolton Wanderers	★★★★	1923, '26, '29, '58
Wolves	★★★★	1893, 1908, '49, '60
West Ham	★★★	1964, '75, '80
Sheffield Wednesday	★★★	1896, 1907, '35
Portsmouth	★★	1939, 2008

Sunderland	🏆🏆	1937, '73
Bury	🏆🏆	1900, '03
Preston	🏆🏆	1889, 1938
Nottingham Forest	🏆🏆	1898, 1959
Old Etonians	🏆🏆	1879, 1882
Wigan	🏆	2013
Wimbledon	🏆	1988
Coventry	🏆	1987
Ipswich	🏆	1978
Southampton	🏆	1976
Leeds	🏆	1972
Blackpool	🏆	1953
Charlton	🏆	1947

RECORD BREAKERS

As you would expect with a competition that's nearly 150 years old, there are stacks of stats and records to reveal about the FA Cup. Check out all this info!

1. Arsenal have played in a record twenty FA Cup finals between 1927 and 2017.

2. Leicester have appeared in a record four FA Cup finals without ever winning.

3. Chelsea striker Didier Drogba scored in four FA Cup finals.

4. The biggest FA Cup scoreline was when Preston beat Hyde 26–0 in 1887.

5. Arsenal manager Arsène Wenger won a record sixth FA Cup in 2015.

6. Scottish team Queen's Park reached the final in 1884 and 1885.

7. Liverpool striker Ian Rush scored five FA Cup final goals.

8. Everton have been unlucky in the FA Cup, losing a record eight finals.

9. Blackburn Rovers are the only club still in existence to win three finals in a row.

10. In 1888, an FA Cup game was played on Christmas Day when Linfield beat Cliftonville 7–0.

FIFA
WORLD CUP

The World Cup finals only happen every four years, but for fans and players it's worth waiting for the greatest football festival on Earth. From Brazil to Belgium, Argentina to Australia and Spain to South Africa — every nation wants that magical gold trophy.

WINNERS

CLUB	WINS	YEARS
Brazil	★★★★★	1958, '62, '70, '94, 2002
Germany	★★★★	1954*, '74*, '90*, 2014
Italy	★★★★	1934, '38, '82, 2006
Argentina	★★	1978, '86
Uruguay	★★	1930, '50
England	★	1966
Spain	★	2010
France	★	1998, 2018

*As West Germany

FOOTY FACT!

The current World Cup trophy was first used in 1974. It's made of gold-plated sterling silver and is 37 centimetres high.

HOW IT WORKS

Countries play qualifying games before the tournament and for the 2018 World Cup in Russia, thirty-two teams reached the finals. After the group stage games, there are three knockout rounds before two teams contest the final.

RECORD BREAKERS

There were 20 World Cup finals between 1930 and 2014. The top scorer at each wins a trophy called the Golden Boot. Listed below are the all-time top scorers at World Cup tournaments.

PLAYER	COUNTRY	WORLD CUP FINALS	GOALS
Miroslav Klose	Germany	2002, '06, '10, '14	16
Ronaldo	Brazil	1994, '98, 2002, '06	15
Gerd Müller	Germany	1970, 1974	14
Just Fontaine	France	1958	13
Pelé	Brazil	1958, '62, '66, '70	12
Sándor Kocsis	Hungary	1954	11
Jürgen Klinsmann	Germany	1990, '94, '98	11
Helmut Rahn	Germany	1954, '58	10
Gary Lineker	England	1986, '90	10
Gabriel Batistuta	Argentina	1994, '98, 2002	10
Teófilo Cubillas	Peru	1970, '78, '82	10
Thomas Müller	Germany	2010, '14	10
Grzegorz Lato	Poland	1974, '78, '82	10

WINNERS AND LOSERS

Germany has scooped four World Cups, but they've also lost the final four times. As West Germany they lost in 1966, 1982 and 1986 and the unified German team were beaten by Brazil in 2002. In 2018, they went out at group stage.

FOOTY FACT!

Germany's Lothar Matthäus and Mexico's Antonio Carbajal are the only two players to play at five World Cup finals.

SOUTH AMERICAN ★ ★
COPA AMÉRICA

The Copa America is South América's equivalent of the Euros and is the oldest international competition in the world. There have been forty-four competitions between 1916, when it first started, and 2017. There are now twelve teams that compete in group games and knockout stages, with Uruguay holding the record for the most wins.

WINNERS

CLUB	WINS	YEARS
Uruguay	🏆🏆🏆🏆🏆🏆🏆🏆🏆🏆🏆🏆🏆🏆🏆	1916, '17, '20, '23, '24, '26, '35, '42, '56, '59, '67, '83, '87, '95, 2011
Argentina	🏆🏆🏆🏆🏆🏆🏆🏆🏆🏆🏆🏆🏆🏆	1921, '25, '27, '29, '37, '41, '45, '46, '47, '55, '57, '59, '91, '93
Brazil	🏆🏆🏆🏆🏆🏆🏆🏆🏆	1919, '22, '49, '89, '97, '99, 2004, '07, '17
Peru	🏆🏆	1939, '75
Paraguay	🏆🏆	1953, '79
Chile	🏆🏆	2015, '16
Colombia	🏆	2001
Bolivia	🏆	1963

SUPER SANCHEZ

Arsenal forward Alexis Sánchez was Chile's hero in the 2015 Copa América — the first time they won the tournament. He scored the winning penalty in the final shoot-out win against Argentina. Argentina also had Messi in attack but they still couldn't win their first trophy since 1993.

RECORD BREAKERS

As you will have seen in this *Football Handbook*, many of the world's best players have been from South America. Messi, Agüero, Pelé, Maradona and Brazil's Ronaldo have all taken part in this famous tournament. Run your eyes over these cool Copa America stars and statistics...

1. Brazil legend Pelé was the top scorer in the 1959 tournament with eight goals.
2. Uruguay's Barcelona forward Luis Suárez was named the tournament's best player in 2011.
3. Lionel Messi won four Man of the Match awards at the 2015 Copa America.
4. Brazil's Zizinho and Argentina's Norberto Méndez scored a record seventeen Copa America goals.
5. Argentina hosted the Copa América a record nine times between 1916 and 2011.
6. Argentina are also the only country to win three Copa Américas in a row.
7. Chile lost a record eighty-one Copa America games between 1916 and 2015.

FOOTY FACT!

The Copa América trophy is seventy-five centimetres tall and weighs nine kilograms — it's one of the biggest trophies in football.

YEAR WE GO

Unlike the World Cup and Euros, the staging of the Copa América has been very disorganized and irregular. At various times in its long history it has been held annually, then every two, three or four years. For the last few years it has been every three or four years, with tournaments in 2007, 2011, 2015, 2016 and 2017. It's all a bit crazy, but maybe that's part of the appeal of this historical cup!

FOOTY FACT!

A special Copa América was played in 2016 to celebrate 100 years of the tournament.

★★★★★ EUROPEAN ★★★★★ CHAMPIONSHIP

Between World Cup tournaments, and held every four years, are the European Championships. Better known as the Euros, the best teams in the continent battle to qualify for the three-week long contest, where they then play group games and knockout games. Take a look at the tournament's history...

WINNERS

CLUB	WINS	YEARS
Germany	🏆🏆🏆	1972*, 80*, 96
Spain	🏆🏆🏆	1964, 2008, 2012
France	🏆🏆	1984, 2000
Soviet Union	🏆	1960
Italy	🏆	1968
Czech Republic	🏆	1976
Netherlands	🏆	1988
Denmark	🏆	1992
Greece	🏆	2004
Portugal	🏆	2016

*As West Germany

EPIC EXPANSION

Just four teams — the Soviet Union, Yugoslavia, Czechoslovakia and France — competed in the first Euros finals. The tournament expanded to eight teams in 1980, sixteen in 1996 then twenty-four teams took part in Euro 2016 in France. The host country always qualifies automatically, just like England did when they hosted Euro 96.

NUMBER CRUNCHER

The Euros have become a major international sporting event, with nearly 1.5 million fans watching live games and 300 million people watching the Euro 2012 final on TV. This guide has crunched some numbers and revealed these amazing facts...

1. When Spain won the Euro 2012, they conceded just one goal in the finals.
2. England hold the record of appearing in nine finals between 1968 and 2012 without ever being champions.
3. In 2012, Holland's Jetro Willems became the youngest tournament player aged eighteen years and seventy-one days.
4. Cristiano Ronaldo was the youngest player to appear in a final. He was nineteen years and 150 days at Euro 2004.
5. Spain were the first team to win two tournaments in a row, in 2008 then 2012.
6. In the first sixteen finals, Euro 2000 held the record of seeing the most goals scored in a tournament with 85.
7. Giovanni Trapattoni was the oldest coach at the Euros. He was seventy-three years and ninety-three days when he managed Republic of Ireland in 2012.
8. Between 1960 and 2012, Yugoslavia were the only team to appear in two finals and never win one.

FOOTY FACT!

The Euro trophy is called the Henri Delaunay Trophy and is named after a former UEFA General Secretary.

PERFECT PLATINI

When France won Euro 84, Michel Platini scored two 'perfect' hat-tricks in the group stage. That means he scored with his left foot, his right foot and his head.

MORE TOP
COMPETITIONS

ASIAN CUP

This is the biggest international women's competition for countries in the Asian Football Confederation. China lead the way with eight final wins, including seven in a row between 1986 and 1999. There have been nineteen events since the first in 1975 and women now compete for the trophy every four years. The Japanese women's team finally won it in 2014 after a record four defeats in the final.

GERMAN BUNDESLIGA

Some people say the German league lacks the glamour of England, Spain and Italy. But have those people ever been to a Bundesliga game? The clubs are huge, the players are top class and the atmosphere is electric! The German Bundesliga was created in 1963 and it was the first time there was a professional top-level league. Bayern Munich have won the most league titles ... by a mile! In 2012, Bayern Munich broke the Bundesliga transfer record when they spent £31.6 million on Athletic Bilbao midfielder Javi Martínez.

UEFA WOMEN'S CHAMPIONSHIP

This women's competition began in 1984, with only four countries — Sweden, England, Denmark and Italy — taking part. Between then and 2017, twelve finals have taken place with Germany dominating with eight wins. Germany won six finals in a row and famously beat England 6–2 in the 2009 final. The tournament is now held every four years and in 2017, sixteen countries competed for the trophy in the Netherlands, with the host country's team taking the top spot.

The popular EA Sports FIFA football computer game involved female players for the first time in the FIFA 16 version.

FOOTY FACT!

CONCACAF WOMEN'S CHAMPIONSHIPS

The USA Women's international team rules the CONCACAF Gold Cup, which is a competition for countries from North America, Central America and the Caribbean. The Americans were the first winners in 1991, beating Canada 5–0, and then won six of the next eight competitions. Surprisingly, world footy giants Brazil have never won it — their best finish was as runners-up in 2000.

SUPER STEPH!

Full name: Stephanie Jayne Houghton
Born: 23 April 1988
Position: defender
Clubs: Man City, England
Country: England
Famous for: scoring goals in all three group-stage matches at the 2012 Olympics

Talented defender and cool-headed Houghton is an inspiration to young footballers both on and off the pitch. She led the Three Lionesses to third place in the 2016 World Cup and received and MBE for services to football.

COMPETITIONS QUIZ

With a stack of knowledge about world tournaments, can you crack the answers to these questions?

TROPHY TALK

Look at these shiny pieces of silverware, then write the names of each trophy.

1.

2.

3.

_____   _____   _____

4.

5.

_____   _____

CHAMP OR CHUMP?

Put a tick or cross next to these players if they have won the Champions League.

WAYNE ROONEY ☐

THEO WALCOTT ☐

LUIS SUÁREZ ☐

JAMES MILNER ☐

PAOLO MALDINI ☐

CUP SWITCH

This trophy was the original trophy awarded in a famous tournament, but which competition was it?

Answers on page 93

EPIC MOMENTS

What? Rooney becomes England's record goalscorer

When? September 2015

On September 8 2015, Wayne Rooney scored for England against Switzerland. It was his 50th international goal, which meant he became the all-time top scorer for the country. Bobby Charlton held the 49-goal record since 1970.

TOP 10 STADIUMS

The atmosphere, the noise, the singing, the colour — football stadiums are famous for all these things on match days. Watching a game at any stadium is a brilliant experience, but if you're lucky enough to be at one of these top-ten stadiums it will be even more special!

10

OLD TRAFFORD

Club: Manchester United
Country: England
Year built: 1910
Capacity: 74,994

Nicknamed The Theatre Of Dreams, Old Trafford has been home to some incredible players and teams, and thrilling games over the last 100 years. It's one of the biggest capacity club stadiums in the UK and was a fortress for Manchester United as they dominated the first twenty years of the Premier League.

9

With its eleven concrete towers and famous red girders sticking out, Italy's largest stadium is easily recognized. It hosted games in the 1990 World Cup and staged the 2016 Champions League final. Since 1947, Milan rivals AC and Inter have shared the ground — these 'derby' games at the San Siro are very passionate!

SAN SIRO

Club: Inter Milan & AC Milan
Country: Italy
Year built: 1926
Capacity: 80,018

8

STADIO OLIMPICO

Club: Roma and Lazio
Country: Italy
Year built: 1937
Capacity: 72,698

World Cup finals, Champions League finals, Coppa Italia finals — Rome's Olympic Stadium has seen lots of action. With its iconic running track separating the pitch from the fans, it certainly looks different to more modern grounds. When city rivals Roma and Lazio contest each other, the atmosphere is red hot.

7

SIGNAL IDUNA PARK

Club: Borussia Dortmund
Country: Germany
Year built: 1974
Capacity: 81,360

More commonly known as the Westfalenstadion, Borussia Dortmund's towering ground is the biggest in Germany. Its most famous fact is that the South Terrace holds nearly 25,000 standing spectators, making it the largest stand in Europe — and probably the noisiest too!

6

ALLIANZ ARENA

Club: Bayern Munich and TSV 1860 Munich
Country: Germany
Year built: 2005
Capacity: 75,000

The Allianz Arena is one of the most advanced stadiums ever — at night its exterior can even change colour! Its clever construction from 2,874 air-filled plastic panels means it's unlike any other stadium and, when it's shining bright, it can even be seen fifty miles away in Austria.

Called 'The Chocolate Box' because of its flat stand on one side and three steep, curved stands. Many fans say the atmosphere, noise and singing at this famous South American ground is the best in the world — other teams certainly don't enjoy battling Boca Juniors here.

5

LA BOMBONERA

Club: Boca Juniors
Country: Argentina
Year built: 1940
Capacity: 49,000

4

MARACANÃ

Club: Flamengo and Fluminense
Country: Brazil
Year built: 1950
Capacity: 78,838

Built for the 1950 World Cup final, which hosts Brazil lost to Uruguay, the Maracanã is a breath-taking football stadium that attracts fans from all over the globe. It was rebuilt for the 2014 World Cup, but still remains as sacred as ever to Brazilians.

3

BERNABÉU

Club: Real Madrid
Country: Spain
Year built: 1947
Capacity: 81,044

Cristiano Ronaldo, Raúl, Alfredo di Stéfano, Hugo Sánchez – all these football legends have been lucky to call the Bernabéu their home. It has staged World Cup and Champions League finals and its luxurious detail and seating befits a super-stylish Spanish club like Real Madrid.

2

CAMP NOU

Club: Barcelona
Country: Spain
Year built: 1957
Capacity: 99,354

Barcelona's Lionel Messi is perhaps the greatest player ever, and the Camp Nou stadium he graces is probably the greatest club ground on the planet. With the largest capacity in Europe, and the traditional purple and blue of the Barça kit shouting loud from every stand, an away trip to the Camp Nou is a total treat for visiting fans. Hundreds of people even tour its museum every day.

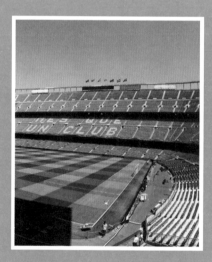

FOOTY FACT!

In the 1982 World Cup tournament in Spain, the Camp Nou's capacity was a huge 121,401 spectators.

WEMBLEY STADIUM

The No.1 stadium has to be London's Wembley. The current stadium was built on the site of the famous original ground, which was knocked down in 2001, and the modern version remains just as iconic to football fans all over the world. It now has a partially retractable roof and a 134-metre high arch which spans the ground and lights up at night. Every player dreams of victory at Wembley!

Club: No club attached
Country: England
Year built: 2007
Capacity: 90,000

FOOTY FACT!

The stadium cost a huge £757 million when it was constructed between 2001 and 2007.

You've toured super stadiums around the world, so now you can take on this super quiz...

YOU'RE GROUNDED

Choose the correct route — A, B, C, or D?

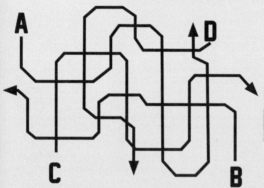

STADIUM SWAP

Rearrange these letters to reveal a famous ground.

DAFT LORD FOR

WORD FIT

Five of the top-ten stadium names fit into this grid. We've given you some letters to help — just fill in the rest.

CAMP NOU   WEMBLEY   SAN SIRO   BERNABEU
~~SIGNAL IDUNA PARK~~

★ FINAL FOOTY ★
QUIZ

Can you answer all these tough footy teasers? Get cracking and see just how much you know!

WORLD CUP WONDERS

How many times have these countries won the World Cup?
Draw a line to the right number.

BRAZIL   2
GERMANY   1
FRANCE   4
ARGENTINA   5

TROPHY TEST

Which trophies are these players holding?

A. Verónica Boquete, FFC Frankfurt

1. Women's Bundesliga

B. Melanie Behringer, Bayern Munich

2. Women's World Cup

C. Abby Wambach, USA

3. Women's Champions League

FOOTY WORDSEARCH

Take a look for these eleven footy words hidden in the grid.

M	A	E	T	N	Z	O	Y	T	R	E	L	A	O	G
A	R	S	P	F	A	K	O	X	B	Q	J	P	C	Z
R	E	E	U	R	K	R	Y	A	L	U	K	O	R	H
A	F	D	F	A	I	O	F	D	L	O	T	R	Z	M
C	E	I	Y	K	C	I	R	T	T	A	H	A	A	S
O	R	S	D	E	K	G	Z	H	R	Q	F	Y	T	D
M	E	F	T	R	O	P	H	Y	U	D	E	A	N	A
P	E	F	C	T	F	B	T	L	C	A	D	V	O	N
E	Q	O	P	R	F	A	J	S	K	I	L	Z	T	O
T	A	Z	B	U	S	S	A	S	U	C	R	N	K	G
I	B	C	O	A	E	P	U	M	S	S	Z	I	A	P
T	J	R	E	D	L	S	Z	A	C	I	G	G	E
I	F	X	U	E	E	J	A	S	S	K	O	C	E	L
O	H	R	R	E	K	I	R	T	S	A	X	T	F	L
N	A	C	T	A	C	K	L	E	O	Z	K	J	T	E

COMPETITION	OFFSIDE	STRIKER	GOAL
TROPHY	KICK OFF	HAT TRICK	REFEREE
TACKLE	STADIUM	TEAM	

Answers on page 93

EPIC MOMENTS

What? Vardy scoring for 11 games in a row
When? November 2015
Leicester striker Jamie Vardy celebrated scoring in a record 11 Premier League games in a row after he scored against Man United. His goals in the 2015–16 season helped lead Leicester's surprise charge for the league title.

ANSWERS

PAGES 20-21

GAME OVER: 1B, 2C, 3A

SHIRT SWAP: Goalkeeper – 1, right-back – 2, centre-back – 5, centre-back – 6, left-back – 3, right-winger – 7, central midfielder – 4, central midfielder – 8, left-winger – 11, striker – 9, striker – 10.

SPOT THE DIFFERENCE:

PAGES 42-43

PICK A PLAYER: 1 – C, 2 – A, 3 – C

Award Winner: N'Golo Kanté

NUMBER CRUNCHER: Messi – 10, Neymar – 11, Suárez – 9.

PAGES 54-55

NAME GAME: 1. Paris Saint-Germain, 2. Liverpool, 3. Real Madrid, 4. Bayern Munich, 5. Arsenal Ladies FC

MATCH UP: Manchester United – The Red Devils, Barcelona – Barça, Juventus – The Old Lady, Real Madrid – The Whites, Atlético Madrid – Rojiblancos.

LOOKING FOR LEGENDS WORDSEARCH:

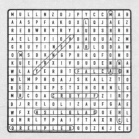

PAGES 78-79

TROPHY TALK: 1. Premier League, 2. Champions League, 3. World Cup, 4. Copa America, 5. FA Cup

CHAMP OR CHUMP? Rooney – ✓, Walcott – X, Suárez – ✓, Milner – X, Maldini – ✓.

CUP SWITCH: World Cup (Jules Rimet trophy).

PAGES 88-89

YOU'RE GROUNDED: route C

STADIUM SWAP: Old Trafford

WORD FIT: 1. Camp Nou , 2. San Siro, 3. Bernabéu, 4. Signal Iduna Park, 5. Wembley.

PAGES 90-91

WORLD CUP WONDERS: Brazil – 5, Germany – 4, Argentina – 2, France –1

TROPHY TEST: A – 3, B – 1, C – 2.

FOOTY WORDSEARCH:

INDEX

A

AC Milan 40, 64–7, 82
Agüero, Sergio 31, 59
Allianz Arena 49, 84
Arsenal 53, 58–9, 68–9, 72
Atlético Madrid 49

B

Bale, Gareth 51
Barcelona 33, 35, 43, 50, 56
Bayern Munich 41, 49, 76, 84
Beckham, David 8, 13
Bernabéu 51, 85
Boca Juniors 40, 84
(La) Bombonera 84
Brazil 22, 32, 40, 71, 85
Bronze, Lucy 36
Bruyne, Kevin De 29
Buffon, Gianluigi 48, 65

C

Camp Nou 35, 50, 86
cards (yellow and red) 13
Cavani, Edinson 27
Celtic 67
Champions League 66
Charlton, Bobby 41, 80
Copa America 72
Cruyff, Johan 41

D

Dybala, Paulo 28

E

European Championship 74

F

FA Cup 68

G

Gea, David De 29
Golden Boot 18, 71

H

Harder, Pernille 36
Hazard, Eden 28

I

Ibrahimovic, Zlatan 8, 47
Iniesta, Andrés 50
Isco 26

J

Juventus 48, 59, 64

K

Kane, Harry 24
Kanté, N'Golo 30
Kerr, Samantha 37
Kroos, Toni 25

L

laws of the game 11
Lewandowski, Robert 31
(La) Liga 59
Liverpool 33, 46, 59
Lloyd, Carli 39

M

Manchester United 34, 41, 47, 59
Maracanã 85
Maradona, Diego 35, 40
Marcelo 30
Marozsán, Dzsenifer 37
Marta 63
Martens, Lieke 38
Matthäus, Lother 6, 49, 71
M'Bappé, Kylan 25
Messi, Lionel 35, 50, 56, 61, 72
Modric, Luka 24
Moore, Bobby 44
Müller, Gerd 41, 49, 71

N

Neymar 32, 43, 47, 50

O

offside rule 13
Old Trafford 47, 82

P

Pelé 8, 71, 73
Platini, Michel 40, 48, 75
Pogba, Paul 48, 59
Premier League 58

R

Ramos, Sergio 27
Real Madrid 51, 60, 67, 85
referee 12
Ronaldo (Brazil) 40, 71
Ronaldo, Cristiano 34, 51, 61
Rooney, Wayne 80

S

San Siro 82
Sánchez, Alexis 51, 72
Scotland vs England 11
Serie A 64
Shearer, Alan 59
Signal Iduna Park 83
Spain 60
Stadio Olimpico 83
Suárez, Luis 33
substitutes 14

U

USA Women 77

V

Vardy, Jamie 92

W

Wembley 87
Women's World Cup 62
World Cup 70

Z

Zidane, Zinedine 38